with the author's respects

AN

ADDRESS

ON THE

LIMITS OF EDUCATION,

READ BEFORE THE

Massachusetts Institute of Technology,

NOVEMBER 16, 1865.

By JACOB BIGELOW, M. D.

BOSTON:
E. P. DUTTON & COMPANY,
135 Washington, corner of School Street.
1865.

AN

ADDRESS

ON THE

LIMITS OF EDUCATION,

READ BEFORE THE

Massachusetts Institute of Technology,

NOVEMBER 16, 1865.

BY JACOB BIGELOW, M. D.

BOSTON:
E. P. DUTTON & COMPANY,
135 WASHINGTON, CORNER OF SCHOOL STREET.
1865.

At a meeting of the MASSACHUSETTS INSTITUTE OF TECHNOLOGY, held on the 16th inst., it was

VOTED, That the thanks of the Institute be presented to DR. BIGELOW, for the interesting and instructive Address by him read this evening, and that, with his permission, the same be printed for and at the expense of the Institute.

Attest,

THOMAS H. WEBB, SECRETARY.

HENRY W. DUTTON & SON, PRINTERS,
90 & 92 WASHINGTON STREET.

ADDRESS.

In 1829 a volume was published in Boston bearing the name of "Elements of Technology." This name was not then in use nor was it generally understood, except by those who drew its meaning from its etymology. It was not in Johnson's Dictionary, nor yet in Rees's Cyclopædia. In Worcester's Dictionary, where it now has a place, no older authority is cited for its support than that of the volume alluded to. Its analogue indeed was extant in some other languages, and fifty years ago was published in Latin among the "Theses" of the graduating class of Harvard College. But its revival for the use of English readers had to be justified by the assertion that it might be found in some of the older dictionaries.

Such, less than forty years ago, was the doubtful tenure in English literature of a word which now gives name in this city to a vigorous and popular institution, a large endowment, a magnificent edifice, and at the same time a great and commanding department of scientific study in every quarter of the civilized world.

It has happened in regard to technology that in the present century and almost under our own eyes, it has advanced with greater strides than any other agent of civilization, and has done more than any science to enlarge the boundaries of profitable knowledge, to extend the dominion of mankind over nature, to economize and utilize both labor and time, and thus to add indefinitely to the effective and available length of human existence. And next to the influence of Christianity on our moral nature, it has had a leading sway in promoting the progress and happiness of our race.

To appreciate what has been done by the applied sciences operating through their dependent and associate arts, we have only to go back a little more than two thirds of a century, to the times of Franklin and Washington, and in many cases to those of our own immediate fathers. In those days of small things, men were compelled to pass their lives in a sort of destitution which in this age of scientific luxury would be considered a state of semi-barbarism. The means of domestic convenience, personal neatness, easy locomotion, rapid intelligence, agreeable warmth, abundant light, physical as well as intellectual, were things wished and waited for, but not yet found.

To us, their effeminate descendants, it might be painfully interesting to witness the efforts of those hardy and much enduring people to procure warmth in their dwellings, by the scorching and freezing of their alternate sides, under the blast that swept from many apertures towards the current of a vast open chimney. And this state of things was hardly bettered by the established zero temperature of an unwarmed church, or the irrespirable atmosphere of a stove-heated school room or country court house. Our recent progenitors read their dusky and infrequent newspaper by the light of a tallow candle, and groped their way through dark and unpaved streets under the guidance of a peripatetic lantern. If in summer they desired a draught of cold water, there was no ice; and if in winter they wished for dry feet, there was no India rubber. If in darkness they sought for light, there was neither gas nor even lucifer matches.

Men were stationary in their habits and deliberate under their necessities. He who would communicate with a friend in a neighboring State might do it in a week, provided he could devote a preparatory week to seeking a safe private conveyance. And if any one had occasion to transport himself from one town or city to another, he could do it on a trusty saddle horse, or still more rapidly in the organized relays of the Boston and New York stage coach "Despatch Line," which undertook to put him through in less than a week. They who went down to the sea in ships could reach England from either of the above named ports in from one to two months if wind and weather were favorable. Literary productions were written out with a goosequill, and printed in a reasonable time by the labor of two men toiling at a hand press. Housewives plied the spinning-wheel, the distaff and the shuttle, and webs of coarse texture grew into perceptible existence with a speed which might be compared to that of a growing vegetable. Beef was roasted on a revolving spit, turned round by a man, a dog, or a smoke jack. And what will hereafter be accounted still more strange, garments were made by sewing slowly together their constituent parts with a needle and thread.

I have taken technology as a leading exponent of the great advance which was to be made, and has been made, during the lifetime of some of us, in certain intellectual and practical improvements of mankind, in supplying the wants, overcoming the difficulties and increasing the elegances of life. To enumerate all these improvements would simply be to recount the great steps by which our own age has advanced to the elevated and privileged condition in which we now see it. And yet, although the practical arts, in the hands of science, have taken the lead in the great visible changes of the present century, it would be presumptuous to call technology the only field from the cultivation of which mankind have obtained abundant and unlooked for harvests. In every other walk or sphere of science, literature and refined humanity, the civilized world, with unfaltering progress, has pushed forward, at the same time, its dominion over mind and matter.

It is the object of the present remarks to show that the amount of knowledge appropriate to civilization which now exists in the world is more than double, and in many cases more than tenfold, what it was about half a century ago, and that therefore no individual can expect to grasp in the limits of a lifetime even an elementary knowledge of the many provinces of old learning, augmented as they now are by the vast annexations of modern discovery. Still farther, education which represents the threshold of accessible knowledge, instead of being expanded, must be contracted in the number and amount of its requirements, so that while all its doors are freely kept open to those who possess time, opportunity and special aptitude or necessity, a part of them at least must be closed to those who do not possess those requisites. If in the days of the ancient Greeks "life was short," while "art was long," how is it now, when life is not longer, but art, literature and science are immeasurably greater? How will it be in another half century, when new discoveries shall have arisen commensurate in their results with those of electro-magnetism and of solar actinism, of modern optical combinations and geographical and geological explorations? How will it be with the discoveries of newly armed astronomers and the calculations of geometers yet to appear, — with revolutions stirred up by chemists among elements that have slumbered together since the creation, — with the augmented conversions of heat into force, driving innumerable mechanisms to minister to man's pleasure and power, — and more than all, how will it be with the cumbrous, vast and insurmountable weight of books, which shall render literary distinction a thing of chance, of uncertainty, perhaps even of impossibility.

A law which obtains in matter, obtains also in regard to the mind and its acquirements, that strength is not increased in proportion to magnitude. The static and dynamic strength of materials for the most part decreases as their bulk increases. A column or a bridge cannot be carried beyond a certain size without crushing or breaking its substance, and a whale, if unsupported by the surrounding water, would die from the pressure of his own weight. A small animal will leap many more times his length than a large one, and the integrity of his slender limbs will not be injured by the exertion. The useful development of a tree is known to be promoted by severe pruning, and where this is impossible, as in primeval forests, the trees prune themselves and attain greater height by the death of their under branches, the insufficient supply of sunlight being monopolized by the upper and dominant members at the expense of the lower. These examples, drawn both from inert and organic matter, may serve to illustrate the corresponding truth that human intellect, though varying in capacity in different individuals, has its limits in all plans of enlargement by acquisition, and that these limits cannot be transcended without aggregate deterioration in distracting the attention, overloading the memory or overworking the brain and sapping the foundations of health.

The school system of New England is at the present moment our glory and our shame. We feel a just pride that among us education is accessible to all, because our public schools are open to the humblest persons. But in our zeal for general instruction, we sometimes forget that a majority of men and women must labor with their hands, that the world may not stand still, and that all may not lose by disuse the power to labor. We cannot train all our boys to be statesmen and divines, nor all our girls to be authors and lecturers or even teachers. We ought not, therefore, to drive them into the false position of expecting to attain by extraordinary effort a place which neither nature nor circumstances have made possible. Many unfortunate children have been ruined for life, in body and mind, by being stimulated with various inducements to make exertions beyond their age and mental capacity. A feeble frame and a nervous temperament are the too sure consequences of a brain overworked in childhood. Slow progress, rather than rapid growth, tends to establish vigor, health and happiness. It has always appeared to me that a desirable and profitable mode of school education would be one in which every hour of study should be offset by another hour of exercise required to be taken in the open air.

To illustrate the impossibility of making any one what may be called a general scholar, we need but to take a slight view of the extent and recent progress of a few of the most familiar and popular sciences at the present day. Let us take geography, which treats of the earth's external structure, and geology which treats of its internal. In the first of these the education of many of the present generation abounded in what are now found to be errors and defects. We were taught that the Andes were the highest mountains of the globe, and the Amazon the longest river. Discoverers had then stopped a thousand miles short of the sources of the Nile and of the Missouri. The Columbia and the Sacramento were geographical myths, while a fabulous Oregon or River of the West was laid down on the maps on the hearsay authority of Carver, displacing what are now the Rocky Mountains, and entering the Pacific Ocean about latitude 43°. The existence of the African Niger was known to the Romans, yet the Royal Geographical Society until 1830 did not know where it reached the ocean, though a hundred Englishmen at various times had laid down their lives in African deserts in fruitless attempts to resolve the mysterious problem. It was not until a still later period that the world knew that there was a continuous Arctic Sea, or any thing like an Antarctic continent.

But if so much has been done in the more difficult and inaccessible parts of our globe, how much more has been achieved in the parts accessible to settlement and cultivation. The American continent, the interior map of which was almost a blank at the close of our Revolution, is now profusely dotted with towns, cities, forts, post offices and rail stations, until the most diligent compiler of a Gazetteer is obliged to pause in despair at the manifest defects of his latest edition.

Geology may be considered as almost a creation of the present age. When Werner visited Paris, in 1802, it could hardly be said to consist of more than insulated observations with a few crude and unsettled theories. But now it has become a great, organized, and overshadowing department of science. In every language of Europe it has its voluminous systems and its unfailing periodicals. Societies of special organization carry forward its labors, and every country of the globe is traversed by its observers and collectors. The shelves of museums are weighed down by its accumulations, and in its palæontology alone the Greek language is exhausted to furnish factitious names for the continually developed species of antecedent creations.

Chemistry in a limited degree appears to have attracted the attention of the ancients, but of their proficiency in this pursuit we know more from their preserved relics and results than from their cotemporaneous records. In modern times the chemists constitute a philosophical community having a language of their own, a history of their own, methods, pursuits and controversies of their own, and a domain which is coextensive with the materials of which our globe is made. Many men of gifted minds and high intellectual attainments, have devoted their lives to the prosecution of this science. Chemistry has unravelled the early mysteries of our planet, and has had a leading agency in changing the arts and the economy of human life. It now fills the civilized world with its libraries, laboratories and lecture-rooms. No individual can expect to study even its accessible books, still less to become familiar with its recorded facts. Yet chemistry is probably in its infancy, and opens one of the largest future fields for scientific cultivation.

Natural history in its common acceptation implies the investigation, arrangement and description of all natural bodies, including the whole organized creation. If no other science existed but this, there would be labor enough and more than enough to employ for life the students and observers of the world. Each kingdom of organic nature already offers to our acquaintance its hundred thousand specific forms, and these are but the vanguard of a still greater multitude believed to cover the surface of countries yet unexplored, and to fill the mysterious recesses not yet penetrated by the microscope. And as far as we know, every one of these organisms, great or small, carries with it its parasites, to which it affords habitation and food, and which may be supposed not only to double but to multiply in an unknown ratio its original numbers. Again, when we reflect that every one of these species has its own anatomy, its physiology, its peculiar chemistry, its habits, its sensations, its modes of reproduction, its nutrition, its duration, its metamorphoses, its diseases and its final mode of destruction, — we may well despair of knowing much of the whole, when a single species might furnish materials of study for a human lifetime.

The foregoing are examples of the claim on our attention and study advanced by a portion only of the progressive sciences. They serve to develop truths and laws appertaining to the material earth, which truths and laws must have existed had there never been minds to study them. The relations of number and figure, the laws of motion and rest, of gravity and affinity, of animal and vegetable life, must have been the same had the dominant race of man never appeared on earth. But there is another extensive class of scientific pursuits, the subjects of which are drawn from his own nature. He has devised metaphysics to illustrate the operations of his own mind. He has introduced ethical and political science to promote order and happiness, and military science to assist for a time at least in destroying both. He has built up history with "her volumes vast," which volumes are as yet a small thing compared with those that are to come. Under the name of news the press daily inundates the world with a million sheets of cotemporaneous history, for history and news, under small qualifications, are identical. The annals of the last four years may deserve as large a place in the attention of mankind as was due when the poet Campbell informed the Egyptian mummy that since his decease, "a Roman empire had begun and ended." The greatest part of what should have been history is unwritten, and of what has been written the greatest part is of little general value. If all that has actually been committed to papyrus, parchment or paper had by chance been preserved from the effects of time and barbarism, the aggregate would be so vast and the interest so little, that the busy world could hardly turn aside for its examination from more absorbing and necessary pursuits.

But the world is not contented with history which states, or professes to state, the progress, arts, dates, successes and failures of distinguished men and nations. It requires further, the supplementary aid of fiction which finds facts, not in testimony, but in probability; not as they are recorded to have happened, but as they ought to have happened under the circumstances and with the actors. Fiction, moreover, not being restrained by the limits of circumstantial truth, is at liberty to seek embellishment from exaggeration, from ornament, from poetry, from dramatic utterance and passionate expression. Hence it has taken the lead in modern literature, and it is not probable that at this day the most accomplished bibliographer or bookseller could point the way to one-half of its multiplied and perishable productions.

There is neither time nor inducement to refer to the pseudo-sciences, which in all ages have made serious drafts upon the limited lifetime of man, nor to the ephemeral and unprofitable issues which consume his time and labor and wear out his strength. At the present day we have not much to fear from alchemy, palmistry or astrology, nor yet from spiritualism, homœopathy or mormonism. But it is not easy to prevent men from wasting their time in the pursuit of shadows, from substituting exceptions for general laws, from believing things, not because they are probable, but because they are wonderful and entertaining. Still less can we divert them from yielding to the guidance of an excited will, from following prejudices or creating them, from adopting one side of a controversy or party strife for no better reason than that some other party has adopted the opposite.

It would be unnecessary to add to what has already been said, even an inventory of other studies, which present seducing but interminable claims on the life and labor of man. It would be vain to open the flood gates of philology, and to follow the thousand rills of language which have intersected and troubled each other ever since they left their fountains at Babel. And we pause in humility before the very portals of astronomy, which has revealed to us that we roll and revolve, and perhaps again revolve, around we know not what. And helpless as animalcules on the surface of a floating globule, we are ever striving to see, to explore, and to mark our way through the "starry dust" of infinite space. Strong and devoted minds have piled up unreadable tomes, the result of their life-long studies and observations, yet few, save the professional and the initiated, attempt to invade the recondite sanctuary of their deposit.

Thus the immense amount of knowledge, general and special, true and fictitious, salutary and detrimental, the record of which is already in existence, has grown into an insurmountable accumulation, a *terra incognita*, which from its very magnitude is inaccessible to the inquiring world. Hence the economy of the age has introduced the labor-saving machinery of periodical literature, which, by substituting compendiums and reviews for the more bulky originals, has seemed to smooth the up-hill track of knowledge and lighten the Sisyphean load of its travellers. But periodical literature, useful or frivolous as it may be, and indispensable as it undoubtedly is, has become by its very success inflated to an enormous growth, and bids fair in its turn to transcend the overtaxed powers of attention of those for whose use it is prepared. Like our street cars, while it helps forward to their destination a multitude of struggling pedestrians, it substitutes pressure for exercise, and does not save the fatigue of those who are still obliged to stand that they may go. In looking forward to another century, it is curious to consider who will then review the reviews, and condense, redact and digest the compends of compendiums from which the life has already been pressed out by previous condensation.

Since these things are so, — since in the dying words of Laplace, "The known is little, but the unknown is immense," and

> "Since life can little more supply
> Than just to look about us and to die,"

it is a question of paramount importance, how in this short period education can be made to conduce most to the progress, the efficiency, the virtue, and the welfare of man.

It is not presumptuous to say that education to be useful must, as far as possible, be made simple, limited, practicable, acceptable to the learner, adapted to his character and wants, and brought home to his particular case by *subdivision* and *selection*. What is now called a liberal education is a term which means something and nothing. Among us it generally implies an attendance for four years upon the "curriculum" or course of studies prescribed and pursued in some incorporated college or university. This attendance may be punctual and thorough, or it may be negligent and unprofitable, so that while one student makes a limited acquirement of multifarious knowledge, another forgets a great part of what he knew on entering the college, and prepares to forget the rest as soon as he enters upon active life.

Subdivision and selection afford the principal avenues through which men arrive at success in the humbler as well as the more conspicuous walks of life. The mechanical labor of artisans is best performed, and its best results obtained, by distributing its duties among a multitude of special agents, and this is more or less successfully done in proportion as a society, or a craft, is more or less perfectly organized. So likewise in the higher or more intellectual pursuits of life, in which men procure bread by the labor of their heads instead of their hands, the number of learned professions has been within a short time wonderfully increased. In the days of our fathers the learned professions were accounted three in number, — Law, Physic, and Divinity. But now more than three times that number afford means of honorable subsistence to multitudes of duly educated persons. We have now a profession of authors, of editors, of lecturers, of teachers, of engineers, of chemists, of inventors, of architects and other artists; and to these may be added the better class of soldiers and politicians. And all these professions are again subdivided in proportion as society advances in its requirements.

For precisely the same reason that it would not be profitable for experts in a mechanical vocation to distract and dissipate their attention among pursuits alien to their tastes and qualifications, it can hardly be advantageous for pupils and neophytes in learning, to undertake to make themselves competent representatives of the various sciences, the literary studies, the languages, dead and living, which are now professedly taught in our colleges and seminaries. Every individual is by nature comparatively qualified to succeed in one path of life, and comparatively disqualified to shine in another. The first step in education should be for the parties most interested, to study, and as far as possible to ascertain, the peculiar bent and capacity of a boy's mind. This being done, he should be put upon a course of intellectual and physical training corresponding, as far as possible, to that for which nature seems to have designed him. But in all cases a preparatory general elementary education, such as is furnished by our common schools, must be made a prerequisite even to qualify him to inquire. The more thorough this preparatory training is made, the better it is for the student. But after this is completed a special or departmental course of studies should be selected, such as appears most likely to conduct him to his appropriate sphere of usefulness. Collateral studies of different kinds may always be allowed, but they should be subordinate and subsidiary, and need not interfere with the great objects of his especial education.

A common college education now culminates in the student becoming what is called a master of arts. But this in a majority of instances means simply a master of nothing. It means that he has spent much time and some labor in besieging the many doors of the temple of knowledge, without effecting an entrance at any of them. In the practical life which he is about to follow he will often have occasion to lament, be he ever so exemplary and diligent, that he has wasted on subjects irrelevant to his vocation, both time and labor, which, had they been otherwise devoted, would have prepared and assisted him in the particular work he is called on to do.

Young men, as well as their parents in their behalf, are justly ambitious of a collegiate education. Older men often regret that they have not had the opportunity to receive it when young. And this is because of the generally acknowledged fact, that four years, spent under the tuition of faithful, accomplished and gentlemanly teachers, can hardly fail to improve their character, language and bearing, as well as their store of useful knowledge. It is the habitual contact and guidance of superior minds, as well as the progressive attrition with each other, which make young men proficients in rectitude, in honor, in science, in polite literature, in tact, and in manners. And this result will appear, whether they have been taught French at West Point, or Greek in Harvard or Yale.

It is the province of the Institute of Technology, so largely and liberally sustained by the Legislature, by the munificence of individuals, and by the untiring labors of its distinguished president, to endeavor within its sphere to assist in providing for the educational wants of the most practical and progressive people that the world has seen. By its programme of instruction a separate path is provided for all who require to accomplish themselves in any one or more of the especial branches of useful knowledge. It would not be just to ignore the fact that the same thing has long been doing in several of our larger universities, where the practical sciences and the modern languages are extensively taught. But these time-honored institutions exceed some of their younger associates in this respect, that under the name of classical literature they premise and afterwards carry on a cumbrous burden of dead languages, kept alive through the dark ages and now stereotyped in England by the persistent conservatism of a privileged order. I cannot here say much to add to the lucid, scholarly and convincing exposition of the state of education as it now is in the great schools of England, given in a recent lecture before this Institute, by one of its professors, on the subject of classical and scientific studies.* No one who examines this discourse can fail to be impressed with the injudicious exactions made in favor of the dead languages in the English schools and universities, their superfluity as means of intellectual training, and their limited applicability to the wants of the present advanced generation.

I would not underrate the value or interest of classical studies. They give pleasure, refinement to taste, breadth to thought, and power and copiousness to expression. Any one who in this busy world has not much else to do, may well turn over by night and by day the "exemplaria Græca." But if, in a practical age and country, he is expected to get a useful education, a competent living, an enlarged power of serving others, or even of saving them from being burdened with his support, he can hardly afford to surrender four or five years of the most susceptible part of life to acquiring a minute familiarity with tongues which are daily becoming more obsolete, and each of which is obtained at the sacrifice of some more important science or some more desirable language. It may not be doubted that a few years devoted to the study of Greek will make a man a more elegant scholar, a more accomplished philologist, a more accurate and affluent writer, and, if all other things conspire, a more finished orator. But of themselves they will not make him what the world now demands, a better citizen, a more sagacious statesman, a more far-sighted economist, a more able financier, a more skilful engineer, manufacturer, merchant, or military commander. They will not make him a better mathematician, physicist, agriculturist, chemist, navigator, physician, lawyer,

* Professor W. Atkinson.

architect, painter, or musician. The ancient Greeks knew but little, though they knew how to express that little well. The moderns know a great deal more, and know how to express it intelligibly. Antiquity has produced many great men. Modern times have produced equally great men, and more of them.

It is common at the present day to say that the Greek language disciplines the mind, extends the compass and application of thought, and that, by its copiousness, and by its versatility of inflection and arrangement it trains the mind to a better comprehension of words, thoughts, and things. All this is no doubt true, and might have great weight as a governing motive in education, were it not that the same ends can be more cheaply obtained by the agency of other means. Unfortunately for the supremacy of classical literature, all civilized countries are at this moment full of distinguished men and women who write well and speak well, and who have never acquired the learned languages. It is easy to say that such persons would have been more distinguished if they had known the classics. It is easy to say that Laplace would have been a better mathematician, and Faraday a better chemist, if by chance they had been duly instructed in Greek. But this is gratuitous assumption. The contrary result is more probable, inasmuch as the pursuit of classical literature would have abstracted just so much time from more pertinent and profitable investigations. At this day nobody believes that Watt would have made a better steam engine, or Stephenson a better locomotive, if they had been taught philosophy by Plato himself.

The ancient languages, if applied to use, are not adequate to supply the wants of modern cultivation. Truths and things have grown faster than words. Modern customs, arts and sciences can be expressed in French or German, but not in Greek and Latin. A French writer, Professor Goffaux, has undertaken to translate Robinson Crusoe into Latin. The translation is successful as far as easy diction and pure latinity are concerned. But the language of the Romans is at fault in the islands of the Pacific, and new words must be coined to express even imperfectly things which are not coeval with the language employed. The world-renowned "man Friday" is introduced to us under the vicarious name of "Vendredi," and when Friday goes a shooting he loads his "sclopetum" with "pulvis nitralis." If modern Greece should ever become a first-class power among the nations, it will have to complete, as it is now trying to do, a vocabulary of new terms to express the arts and commerce, the facts and fancies, the business and belles lettres of the existing time. In other words, it must reënforce its language with a new half, not found in the ancient classics.

The admiration of the old Romans for the Greek language and literature had its origin in the fact that in that age of limited civilization they found not much else of the kind to admire. They looked to Greece as the fountain of what had been achieved in art, philosophy, poetry and eloquence. Of consequence it was chosen as the great place of resort for educational objects, and Athens became the emporium of literary and philosophic instruction. But the Roman youth would never have been sent to Athens, had there been, as now, a railroad to take them to Paris, or a steamship to bring them to America. They would not have consumed their time in the groves of Academus, if they could have gained admittance to the Ecole Polytechnique, or to the Royal Institution.

At the present day we relish the Greek language, from the mingled impression not only of its own superiority, but of the pleasure it gives us and the pains it has cost us. We relish it as the musician enjoys his music, the mathematician his geometry, and the antiquarian his diggings. We are pleased that it has been preserved with its euphonious intonations, its copious expressiveness, and its noble literature. We know that the spirit of Homer cannot be translated into English, any more than the soul of Shakspeare can be done into Greek. All languages have their idiomatic expressions of thought, and in all of them translation has a killing effect on the strong points of literature. In the opera of Macbetto the term "hell broth" in the witch scene, is rendered in Italian as "polto inferno." And on the opposite page of the libretto, it is served up afresh in English as "infernal soup." It is highly probable that the half savage accomplishments of Homer's heroes and gods cannot be made duly appreciable in the English tongue. Nevertheless, the modern world can get on without them, and we may be excused for believing that if the study of Greek should be abandoned as a requisite in our universities, although it would still be cultivated, like other exceptional studies, with success and delight by a few devotees, yet our practical, bustling and overcrowded generation would never again postpone more useful occupations to adopt it as an indispensable academical study.

In regard to success in the world at the present day, it is not an academic education, however desirable in any shape it may be, that gives a man access to the confidence and general favor of his fellow-men, or to the influential posts of society. It is native talent, reliability, perseverance and indomitable will, that conduct him to the high places of the world. In all countries, and most of all in our own country, a contest continually goes on between academic education and self education, the education that comes from without and the education that comes from within. The much cultivated boy, who under favor of advantages, performs faithfully his allotted tasks, who fulfils the requirements of his teachers, who is accustomed to subordinate his own judgment to the dictation of others; although he may hold a high rank in the scale of proficiency and the amount of acquisition, is liable on arriving at manhood, to continue to lean rather than to lead, and thence to occupy a secondary place in the struggle for worldly distinction. On the other hand, the neglected but independent youth, who is brought up in the suggestive school of necessity, who becomes original and inventive because his life is a continued contest with difficulties, who balances character against opportunity, and individual vigor and patience against external guidance;—such an one from the habit of directing himself becomes more competent to direct others, and to wear more easily offices of trust and responsibility. It is remarkable how many of our distinguished men have been self educated, or at least without academic education. Franklin was a philosopher, Washington a statesman, Patrick Henry an orator, but not by the grace of classical education. Henry Clay knew nothing of the Greek language, nor did probably Thomas Benton. Andrew Jackson and Andrew Johnson had rougher nursing than that of an alma mater. Rumford, Bowditch and Fulton did not develop their intellects under the shades of academic seclusion. And if we were to go abroad for examples, we should find that Napoleon was no classical scholar, and that Peter the Great, when he issued from his lair at Moscow to study the civilization of Western Europe, did not repair to the universities of Cambridge and Oxford, but entered as a working mechanic in the shipyards of Saardam and Deptford.

We need not regret that our country is the field of wholesome competition between the well taught and the self taught, between advantage on the one side and energy on the other, between early development under assistance and slow maturity under difficulties. The success of either condition awakens and stimulates the zeal of the other.

There are many persons who even in this age speak in terms of derogation of what are called utilitarian studies, in contrast with classical and ideal literature, as if pursuits which tend directly to the preservation and happiness of man were less worthy of his attention than those which may be founded in fancy, exaggeration and passion. Poetry, art and fiction have sought for the beautiful and sublime in creations which are imaginary and often untrue, which "o'er inform the pencil and the pen," and attract because they are mysterious and inaccessible. But in the present age, fact has overtaken fancy and passed beyond it. We have no need to create new miracles, nor imagine them, when the appetite for wonder is more than satiated with reality, and objects of delight and amazement confront us in the walks of daily life. I know nothing in nature or art more beautiful than a railroad train, when it shoots by us with a swiftness that renders its inmates invisible, and winds off its sinuous way among mountains and forests, spanning abysses, cleaving hills asunder, and travelling onward to its destination, steadily, smoothly, unerringly, as a migratory bird advances to the polar regions. And I know of nothing more sublime than in the hold of an ocean steamship, to look on the mightiest enginery that has been raised by man, as it wields its enormous limbs like a living thing, and heaves and pants and rolls and plunges — urged onward by the struggling of the imprisoned elements.

The traveller passes daily by the never-ending rows of posts and wires which mark the pathway of the electric telegraph, until at length by their very frequency they are blended in the inert features of the landscape and cease to attract attention. Yet, all the while, invisible thought is riding on those wires, and mind is answering to mind over a thousand miles of distance.

The half fabulous siege of Troy has been made immortal in the epics of Homer and Virgil, and we are led by their poetry to admire the achievements of heathen gods and of heroes descended from them. We stand in awe at the exploits of primitive warriors with the same emotions with which we afterwards mark in history the real deeds and eras of great military commanders. But however much we may be impressed with the imagined spectacle of a host of disciplined barbarians fighting with swords and bucklers, we cannot keep out of sight that they would have been chaff before the wind in the presence of modern military science. Ulysses and Agamemnon were ten years in taking the city of Troy. Ulysses Grant with his batteries would have taken it in ten minutes. Artists, historians and poets depict even now the memorable battles of Alexander and Cæsar. But half a dozen shells would have scattered the Macedonian phalanx, and the Roman Empire could not have stood many days after a modern war steamer should have found its way up the Tiber.

The march of military improvement has not yet halted in its course. The great war of American conservation has been eminently a war of science, and has changed by its inventions the whole face of modern conflicts. Huge forts and strong war ships no longer protect harbors from the inroads of invulnerable enemies. The wooden walls of England, so long her defence and her boast, like the walls of Jericho, have fallen flat before the sound of the distant crashing of rams and monitors and torpedoes. If the time shall ever come when classical readers shall tire at the monotonous championship of Trojans, Greeks and Rutulians, they will kindle with wonder over that miracle of romance and reality, "The Bay Fight" of Mobile, by Henry Howard Brownell.

It is the duty of educational institutions to adapt themselves to the wants of the place and time in which they exist. It needs no uncommon penetration to see that we are now living in a great transition period, and that the world is resting its future hopes, and quieting its future fears in reliance on an educated and enlightened democracy. When Andrew Johnson, at the inauguration ceremony of 1865, somewhat hastily declared himself a plebeian, dependent on the will of the people, and applied the same impeachment to his fellow functionaries, — like Paul of old, he was not mad, but spoke forth the words of truth and soberness. The last few years of history, the greatest and most momentous that the world has ever witnessed, bear testimony to the power of an educated common people, to perceive and to carry forward their own true interests. Against the wiles of an astute and determined oligarchy, against the frowns of foreign privileged orders, amid the vicissitudes of good and evil fortune, this great people have advanced to their final triumph, not of revolution but of conservation, under the guidance of men like themselves, of men who had been cleavers of wood and sewers of garments, who had wrought as farmers, as tanners, and as homely manufacturers, who knew the genius and character of their constituents and the roads through which they were to be conducted to natural and necessary success.

At this moment no nation of the globe can be called more truly powerful than one which has peacefully absorbed into its interior depths half a million of veterans, with discipline in their history, arms in their hands and education in their heads. The most formidable ruler whom the world now knows, is a self-educated man, who could hardly read and write at the age of twenty.

It is a fact so generally admitted, in this country at least, as to have become almost a truism, that prescriptive and hereditary positions are declining in social influence. Personal unworthiness or incompetency cannot be covered up by personal privilege. It is better to be the founder of a great name, than its disreputable survivor. When a marshal of France, Duke of Abrantes and Governor of Paris, was reminded by others of the obscurity of his birth, he proudly replied, "*Moi je suis mon ancetre*," (I am my own ancestor).

In this great and original country, which is now treading in the van of a new reformation, we have thousands yet untaught, who are to become ancestors in fame, ancestors in fortune, ancestors in science, ancestors in virtue. May their descendants be worthy of them.

These are the men who may well claim to "constitute a State." They are, as it were, the granite substratum which underlies the rich coal fields and the arable soils of the earth's exterior surface. Like that they will last when softer and richer tracts shall have been swept away. Yet a continent as extensive and various as ours should be capable of furnishing all soils and materials for all needful and desirable productions. When the necessaries which sustain life are provided, the luxuries which adorn and gratify it must follow in their order. "In every country," says Buckle, "as soon as the accumulation of wealth has reached a certain point, the produce of each man's labor becomes more than sufficient for his support; it is no longer necessary that all should work; and there is found a separate class, the members of which pass their lives for the most part in the pursuit of pleasure; a very few, however, in the acquisition and diffusion of knowledge." This statement is a good exposition of the law which rules in the affairs of this country; it contains the danger and the safety, the bane and the antidote, of our social destiny. In a nation in which "the government is made for the people, and not the people for the government," whose fundamental requisite is "the greatest good of the greatest number," education, elementary and practical, such as common schools can furnish, must be made accessible to all who can be withdrawn, either from labor or idleness, for a sufficient time to realize its advantage. Afterwards those whom favor of fortune or strength of will has qualified to approach higher paths of intellectual culture should be encouraged, assisted and excited to enter and occupy either one or many of the more difficult fields of literature and science, preferring those that best harmonize with the adopted path which is to be the occupation of life. And as to the residuary class, not numerous in any country, to whom is left the option of pursuing pleasure or knowledge, it is fortunate when there is judgment enough to perceive that these two objects can be identified in one pursuit. Knowledge is never so successfully cultivated as when it becomes a pleasure, and no pleasure is more permanent than the successful pursuit of knowledge, combined, as it should be, with moral progress. Natural gifts and variations of aptitude qualify men to tread with advantage the special paths of art and science; and such gifts are most frequently born in and with them, and cannot be imparted from without. A musical ear, an artistic eye and a poetic sense are not to be created in any man. We might as well expect to endow him with the sagacity of the hound, the quick ear of the hare, or the lightning sense of danger which preserves and insures the perilous life of the summer insect.

The man of robust though ungainly frame, may make a first-rate laborer; the slender, shy and delicate youth may shine in the walks of literature; the man of strong voice and prompt and comprehensive intellect may take precedence as an orator. But transpose these conditions, and we have a result of mistakes and failures. What God hath put asunder, man cannot well join together.

I have dwelt on the importance of a special and well selected path of study as leading to success in education, and not less in subsequent life. Nevertheless, the necessity of absolute confinement to this path is to be accepted with great modifications. A youth with vigorous and varied powers will not easily restrict himself to a beaten track, but as his mind grows he will become discursive in his aspirations. He will carry along with him, not only the adopted or select pursuit which has enabled him to serve, to impress or to excel others, but he will also be prompted, both before and after he has grown up, to entertain himself and to extend his relations with those who surround him, by devoting his surplus time, which his very success has given him, to the enlargement of his sphere of occupation. Every professional man, however efficient and prosperous he may be in the discharge of his daily routine, must have, if he would not rust, some collateral pursuits, some by-play of life, in which he may recreate himself and keep up a wholesome freshness by intercourse with congenial minds, and at times with the ideal world. Our country has been called in reproach the arena of a cultivated mediocrity. Happy would it be if all mankind could be brought up even to that level. A cultivated mediocrity is the boundless soil from out of which must spring at times the vigorous and favored shoots of genius, sparse and exceptional though they may be, yet sufficient to supply the just needs of mankind, — various and eccentric in their character, yet conspiring to dignify and ennoble our race. Men cannot all be geniuses, yet there are many in whom exist the germs of art, poetry and eloquence, the love of beauty, the sense of the ideal, and the perception of the unseen. These are the men who, when discovered and brought out, delight, attract, and impress the world; who are generally appreciated, though not often followed; whose presence and inspiration are necessary to the enjoyment and the upward progress of the human race. They spread the sails in the adventurous and perilous voyage of life, while others hold the helm and labor at the ropes.

Our country, with its vast territory, its inviting regions, its various population, its untrammelled freedom, looks forward now to a future which hitherto it has hardly dared to anticipate. Let us hopefully await the period when the world shall do homage to our national refinement, as it now does to our national strength; when the column shall have received its Corinthian capital; and when the proportions of the native oak shall be decorated, but not concealed, by the cultivated luxuriance of vines and flowers.

www.ingramcontent.com/pod-product-compliance
Lightning Source LLC
LaVergne TN
LVHW011124110826
845150LV00008B/2247